Try Not To
LAUGH

Bunny Endorsed!

Joke Book
Challenge

Easter Edition

Try Not To Laugh Game Rules

Easy Version

1. Find an opponent or split up into two teams.
2. Team 1 reads a joke to Team 2 from anywhere in the book.
3. The person reading the joke looks right at the opposing person or team and can use silly voices and funny faces if they wish.
4. If Team 2:

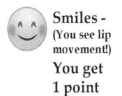 Smiles -
(You see lip movement!)
You get
1 point

 Grins -
(You see teeth!)
You get
2 points

 Laughs -
(You hear noise!)
You get
3 points

5. Read one joke at at time, then switch the giving and receiving teams.
6. The team with most points after five rounds wins! Use the score sheets on the following pages.

Challenge Version

1. Same rules apply except you get one point if you can make the other team laugh. No points for smiling or grinning.

Good luck and try not to laugh!

SCORE SHEET

	TEAM 1	TEAM 2
ROUND 1		
ROUND 2		
ROUND 3		
ROUND 4		
ROUND 5		
TOTAL		

	TEAM 1	TEAM 2
ROUND 1		
ROUND 2		
ROUND 3		
ROUND 4		
ROUND 5		
TOTAL		

	TEAM 1	TEAM 2
ROUND 1		
ROUND 2		
ROUND 3		
ROUND 4		
ROUND 5		
TOTAL		

	TEAM 1	TEAM 2
ROUND 1		
ROUND 2		
ROUND 3		
ROUND 4		
ROUND 5		
TOTAL		

	TEAM 1	TEAM 2
ROUND 1		
ROUND 2		
ROUND 3		
ROUND 4		
ROUND 5		
TOTAL		

	TEAM 1	TEAM 2
ROUND 1		
ROUND 2		
ROUND 3		
ROUND 4		
ROUND 5		
TOTAL		

	TEAM 1	TEAM 2
ROUND 1		
ROUND 2		
ROUND 3		
ROUND 4		
ROUND 5		
TOTAL		

	TEAM 1	TEAM 2
ROUND 1		
ROUND 2		
ROUND 3		
ROUND 4		
ROUND 5		
TOTAL		

SCORE SHEET

	TEAM 1	TEAM 2
ROUND 1		
ROUND 2		
ROUND 3		
ROUND 4		
ROUND 5		
TOTAL		

	TEAM 1	TEAM 2
ROUND 1		
ROUND 2		
ROUND 3		
ROUND 4		
ROUND 5		
TOTAL		

	TEAM 1	TEAM 2
ROUND 1		
ROUND 2		
ROUND 3		
ROUND 4		
ROUND 5		
TOTAL		

	TEAM 1	TEAM 2
ROUND 1		
ROUND 2		
ROUND 3		
ROUND 4		
ROUND 5		
TOTAL		

	TEAM 1	TEAM 2
ROUND 1		
ROUND 2		
ROUND 3		
ROUND 4		
ROUND 5		
TOTAL		

	TEAM 1	TEAM 2
ROUND 1		
ROUND 2		
ROUND 3		
ROUND 4		
ROUND 5		
TOTAL		

	TEAM 1	TEAM 2
ROUND 1		
ROUND 2		
ROUND 3		
ROUND 4		
ROUND 5		
TOTAL		

	TEAM 1	TEAM 2
ROUND 1		
ROUND 2		
ROUND 3		
ROUND 4		
ROUND 5		
TOTAL		

SCORE SHEET

	TEAM 1	TEAM 2
ROUND 1		
ROUND 2		
ROUND 3		
ROUND 4		
ROUND 5		
TOTAL		

	TEAM 1	TEAM 2
ROUND 1		
ROUND 2		
ROUND 3		
ROUND 4		
ROUND 5		
TOTAL		

	TEAM 1	TEAM 2
ROUND 1		
ROUND 2		
ROUND 3		
ROUND 4		
ROUND 5		
TOTAL		

	TEAM 1	TEAM 2
ROUND 1		
ROUND 2		
ROUND 3		
ROUND 4		
ROUND 5		
TOTAL		

	TEAM 1	TEAM 2
ROUND 1		
ROUND 2		
ROUND 3		
ROUND 4		
ROUND 5		
TOTAL		

	TEAM 1	TEAM 2
ROUND 1		
ROUND 2		
ROUND 3		
ROUND 4		
ROUND 5		
TOTAL		

	TEAM 1	TEAM 2
ROUND 1		
ROUND 2		
ROUND 3		
ROUND 4		
ROUND 5		
TOTAL		

	TEAM 1	TEAM 2
ROUND 1		
ROUND 2		
ROUND 3		
ROUND 4		
ROUND 5		
TOTAL		

SCORE SHEET

	TEAM 1	TEAM 2
ROUND 1		
ROUND 2		
ROUND 3		
ROUND 4		
ROUND 5		
TOTAL		

	TEAM 1	TEAM 2
ROUND 1		
ROUND 2		
ROUND 3		
ROUND 4		
ROUND 5		
TOTAL		

	TEAM 1	TEAM 2
ROUND 1		
ROUND 2		
ROUND 3		
ROUND 4		
ROUND 5		
TOTAL		

	TEAM 1	TEAM 2
ROUND 1		
ROUND 2		
ROUND 3		
ROUND 4		
ROUND 5		
TOTAL		

	TEAM 1	TEAM 2
ROUND 1		
ROUND 2		
ROUND 3		
ROUND 4		
ROUND 5		
TOTAL		

	TEAM 1	TEAM 2
ROUND 1		
ROUND 2		
ROUND 3		
ROUND 4		
ROUND 5		
TOTAL		

	TEAM 1	TEAM 2
ROUND 1		
ROUND 2		
ROUND 3		
ROUND 4		
ROUND 5		
TOTAL		

	TEAM 1	TEAM 2
ROUND 1		
ROUND 2		
ROUND 3		
ROUND 4		
ROUND 5		
TOTAL		

What does a bunny use when he goes swimming?
A hare-net.

Why doesn't the Easter Bunny get candy at the movie theater?
Because of the price-- they're always raisinette!

Where does the Easter Bunny like to eat breakfast?
IHOP.

Why did the Easter egg hide?
He was a little chicken.

What do you get if you take your rabbits to Arizona for the summer?
Hot cross bunnies.

What is the Easter Bunny's favorite state capital?
Albunny, New York.

Who delivers chocolate treats to all the fish in the sea?
The Oyster Bunny.

What do you get when you cross a bunny with an onion?
A bunion.

What's the Easter Bunny's favorite type of story?
A cotton tale.

What do you get if you cross an elephant with a rabbit?
An elephant who never forgets to eat his carrots.

Where does Dracula keep his Easter candy?
His Easter casket.

What happened to the Easter Bunny after he misbehaved at school?
He was egg-spelled.

What kind of jewelry does the Easter Bunny wear?
14-carrot gold.

What do you get if you cross a bee and a rabbit?
A honey bunny.

Where do you find information about eggs?
In the hen-cyclopedia.

How do some bunnies commute to work?
The Rabbit Transit.

What do you call the Easter Bunny after Easter?
Tired.

What do you call ten rabbits marching backwards?
A receding hairline.

What happened to the
egg when it was
tickled?
It cracked up.

What did the chicken
win at the contest?
A free range rover.

Where does the Easter Bunny get his eggs?
Eggplants.

Knock Knock.
Who's there?
Sherwood.
Sherwood who?
Sherwood like to have an Easter basket like yours!

Why is the letter "A"
like a flower?
A "B" comes after it.

What happened to the
man who swallowed
the food coloring?
**He felt like he dyed a
little inside.**

What is the Easter
Bunny's favorite sport?
Basketball.

Who is the Easter
Bunny's favorite movie
actor?
Rabbit De Niro.

What type of movie is about waterfowl?
A duck-umentary.

What is the difference between a crazy bunny and a counterfeit dollar?
One is bad money and the other is a mad bunny.

What is the Easter
Bunny's favorite dance?
The bunny hop!

What do you call a
mischievous egg?
A practical yolker.

How do you know
when a magician is
mad?
He pulls his hare out.

What kind of egg is
never on time?
A choco-LATE one.

How is the Bunny like
LeBron James?
**They're both famous
for stuffing baskets.**

How many Easter eggs
can you put in an
empty basket?
**Just one. After that,
it's not empty
anymore.**

What's long and stylish
and full of kittens?
The Easter Purr-ade.

What did the tree say
to spring?
What a re-leaf!

How does a rabbit
throw a tantrum?
**He gets hopping
mad.**

Why did the Easter
Bunny have to fire the
duck?
**He kept quacking the
eggs.**

What does the Easter Bunny get for making a basket?
Two points!

What do you call a rabbit with the sniffles?
A runny bunny.

How do you know the Easter Bunny liked his trip?
Because he said it was egg-cellent.

How does the Easter Bunny keep his fur in place?
With hare spray.

Why does Peter Cottontail hop down the bunny trail? **Because he's too young to drive.**

What did one duck say to the other duck that wouldn't go in the water? **"What are you, chicken?"**

How did Antonio like working on the rabbit farm?

He was it was a hare raising experience.

Knock Knock.

Who's there?

Wendy.

Wendy who?

Wendy Easter Bunny coming to town?

How did the Easter Bunny dry himself after getting caught in the rain?
A hare dryer.

Why did the Easter Bunny cross the road?
Because the chickens had his eggs!

What is the Easter
Bunny's favorite type
of music?
Hip hop.

Why won't Easter eggs
go out at night?
**They don't want to
get beat up.**

Why did the Easter Bunny get fired from the chocolate factory?
He was always taking his sweet time.

What did the woman buy a baby chick instead of a baby duck?
Because it was a little cheaper.

What did the eggs do when the light turned green?
They egg-cellerated.

How does the Easter Bunny keep his fur neat?
With a hare brush.

What do you call a
forgetful rabbit?
A hare-brain!

How do you catch a
unique rabbit?
Unique up on it.
What's the best way to
catch a tame rabbit?
**Tame way, you sneak
up on it.**

How long does the spring duck like to party?
Around the cluck.

How does the Easter Bunny travel?
By hare plane.

How did the eggs leave
the highway?
**They went on the
eggs-it ramp.**

What happened when
the Easter Bunny met
the rabbit of his
dreams?
**They both lived
hoppily ever after!**

What does a Boy Scout
bunny like to do?
**Hop little old ladies
cross the street.**

Where does the Easter
Bunny go when he
needs a shampoo?
The hare dressers.

How do you know that carrots are good for your eyes?
There are no rabbits with glasses.

Who is the Easter Bunny's favorite old time TV duo?
Rabbit and Costello.

What is the best way to send a letter to the Easter Bunny?
Hare mail.

What would you get if your crossed a bunny with Chinese food?
Hop Suey.

How do you know if a gardener is good at his job?
He springs into action.

What did the rabbits do after their wedding ceremony?
They went on a bunny-moon.

Why shouldn't you tell an Easter egg a joke?
It might crack up.

What day does an Easter egg hate the most?
Fry-day!

Why are people always tired in April?
Because they just finished a March.

How does Shrek like his eggs?
Ogre easy.

Where does the Easter Bunny go when he needs a new tail? **The re-tail store.**

What do you call a bunny with a large brain? **An egghead.**

What do you call a
sleepy Easter egg?
Egg-zosted.

Knock Knock.
Who's there?
Alma.
Alma Who?
**Alma Easter candy is
gone can I have some
of yours?**

What do you call a
rabbit with fleas?
Bugs Bunny.

What do you call an
egg from outer space?
**An egg-stra
terrestrial.**

What has big ears,
brings Easter candy,
and goes Hippity-
BOOM, Hippity-BOOM,
Hippity-BOOM?
The Easter Elephant.

What's a chicken
farmer's favorite car?
A coupe.

Did you hear about the girl with food coloring all over her hands?
I've been dying to tell you!

How did the egg climb the hill?
He scrambled up.

Why did the Easter Bunny go to the beauty salon?

To get eggs-tensions in his hare.

What kind of beans grow in the Easter Bunny's garden?

Jellybeans

What would you get if you crossed the Easter Bunny with a famous French general?
Napoleon Bunnyparte.

What did the bunny want when he grew up?
To join the Hare Force.

What do you call a movie about a baby hen?
A chick flick.

Did you hear about the 500 hares that escaped from the zoo?
Police are combing the area.

What kind of duck
can't keep his eyes
closed?
A Peking duck.

Who loves to eat lots
at Thanksgiving
dinner?
The Feaster Bunny.

What do you call a
bunny with an A+ test
in his pocket?
A smarty pants.

What do you get when
you cross a rabbit's
foot with poison ivy?
A rash of bad luck.

What does the Easter Bunny say when he burps?
"Eggs-cuse me!"

What season is it when you are on a trampoline?
Spring-time.

Why were the little girls sad after the race?
Because an egg beater.

What is a duck's favorite game to play?
Billiards.

What did one Easter egg say to other Easter egg?
"Have you heard any good yolks lately?"

What are the Easter Bunny's favorite children's books?
The ones with hoppy endings.

How does Easter end?
With an "R".

Why did the chicken cross the playground?
To get to the other slide.

How does the Easter Bunny stay fit?
Eggs-ercise.

Why is the bunny the luckiest animal?
Because it has four rabbit's feet.

What do you call a rabbit that tells good jokes?

A funny bunny.

How can you tell where the Easter Bunny has been?

Eggs marks the spot.

What do you need if your chocolate eggs mysteriously disappear?
A good eggsplanation.

Why do we paint Easter eggs?
Because it's too hard to wallpaper them.

Did you hear about the
Easter Bunny who sat
on a bee?
It's a very tender tail.

What do you get if you
cross a hen with a dog?
Pooched eggs.

What did the rabbit say to the carrot?
"It's been nice gnawing you, but you have to go!"

How does an Easter chicken bake a cake?
From scratch.

How do comedians like their eggs?
Funny side up.

What the Easter Bunny's favorite dance move?

The bunny hop.

Thanks for playing!

Other Try Not To Laugh Joke Book Challenges You Might Like! Find them on Amazon.com!

Made in the USA
Middletown, DE
15 April 2019